Betsy Williams

Are there Fairies at the bottom of Your Garden?

Growing up green
with the fairies

illustrations by
Ned Williams

ARE THERE FAIRIES AT THE
BOTTOM OF YOUR GARDEN?
Growing up Green with the Fairies

ISBN 0-9701611-1-5

Published by Proper Season Press, Andover MA

Visit Betsy's website for more information
about lectures, classes and books.
www.betsywilliams.com
betsy@betsywilliams.com

Table of Contents

Acknowledgments

We want to give a heartfelt "Thank you" to everyone who helped bring this second edition of Are There Fairies at the Bottom of your Garden? to life: Susan Lenoe, for her patient reading and rereading; my sister, Peg Koller, for her wise and thoughtful guidance in helping to refocus the book's theme and Susan Belsinger, for her excellent editing and steady, cheerful encouragement.

Above all, we owe Claire Russell a deep debt of gratitude for guiding, pushing and pulling us into the age of digital publishing. Because of her hard work, steady direction and gentle smile we were able to stumble through the magic forest of new technology to the other side. Thank you, thank you!!

Introduction

I have been fascinated with myths and legends for as long as I can remember. I still have my first book of Greek myths, given to me when I was four years old. I clearly remember sitting at the top of the stairs outside my mother's bedroom looking at its marvelous pictures. I read fairy tales by the hour throughout my childhood. When asked what I wanted to be when I grew up, I solemnly explained that I planned to be an archaeologist so I could hunt for the ruined homes of the gods and goddesses and excavate sites where fairies used to live.

I loved all those old stories and I still do. In fact, my curiosity about the plants mentioned in some of those stories led me to become a gardener. I wanted to grow, taste and smell the flowers and herbs I had read about. Little did I realize how seductive gardening and plant collecting could be! Here I am, decades later, still avidly collecting plants and plant lore, trying to fit the many-faceted scraps of lore together to create a comprehensive picture.

I cannot provide clear answers as to who or what the inhabitants of fairyland are. I can only indicate a path that could lead you to Faërie, the ancient land of enchantment, whose residents have come to be called "fairies." I will share some of the fascinating bits of information about fairies and their ways that lay embedded like tiny, sparkling gems in the fabric of our oldest folktales and legends.

I'll give you suggestions on how to use the stories and legends of garden and wayside fairies to introduce young children to the very real magic of the natural world. Can there be a lovelier or more enticing way to teach children about horticulture, botany, natural science and ecology than to tell them the stories of the fairies who live in each and every garden and wood, and dance joyously in fairy rings on summer nights? What child, after hearing stories about the world of tiny folk who reward you if you are a gentle thoughtful person and treat the world around you kindly, won't want to see the plants those little people loved so? What fun for the adults who tell the stories, and what joy for the children who know those adults! Imagine the benefits the world would reap if we mortals lived in such a way that the fairies returned to the bottom of our gardens.

I will happily tell the story of the creation of the first Faerie Festival at our herb shop in Massachusetts and how that celebration spread around the world. I'll give you tips on how to create your own festive celebration of the fairies.

Should you choose to take the enchanted path that could lead to the mythical land of Faërie, I leave you with the traditional warning given to all about to embark on a magical quest: The inhabitants of Faërie do not always trust mortals. You must remember to tread softly, mind your manners and be unwaveringly honest and trustworthy. Above all, keep your wits about you! You never know what is going to happen next in the magical land of "Once-upon-a-time."

Enjoy,

Betsy

CHAPTER ONE

Growing up Green with the Fairies

"And as the seasons come and go,
here's something you might like to know.
There are fairies everywhere:
under bushes, in the air,
playing games just like you play,
singing through their busy day.

So listen, touch, and look around,
in the air and on the ground.
And if you watch all nature's things,
you might just see a fairy's wing."
Author Unknown

Enchanted by technology and ensnared in schedules, children of the 21st century are becoming dangerously disconnected from the natural world, a world all humans belong to. Garden and woodland fairies, mythical creatures from long ago, can help rescue our children and guide them down the path of growing up green.

Today's kids spend long hours indoors. Millions of very young children spend all day at preschool or in daycare, the slightly older ones attend school and then after-school programs. Their time in managed care often begins with breakfast at school and doesn't end until they are picked up for supper. Many children finish their day watching the flickering screen of a television, computer or video game.

Once upon a time, kids spent hours outdoors by themselves mucking around. Today, they have little unscripted time to roam the neighborhood poking at beetles and watching butterflies, listening to birds, smelling the air, noticing swelling buds opening into blossoms or seeing clouds shape-shift into dragons and faces. Those discoveries are important to human health. They nurture our imaginations. They teach us to focus on the details of life around us. They build strong connections to the natural world which is home to us all. The memories of those moments stay with us, sometimes returning years later to help frame our adult lives.

The early years of childhood are often called the magic years. This is the time when children are actively learning how the world works. As they collect bits of real-world knowledge, young children's imaginations enable them to piece together scenarios that are very real to the child but appear to be magical thinking to adults. What adults call make-believe can be totally true to young children. Children between two and six years old are the perfect age to introduce to the *real* magic world of nature, the world of living, green growing things just outside the door. Stories about garden and woodland fairies are the perfect bridge from the world indoors to a focused fascination with the garden and woods outdoors.

Children love stories. This makes reading or telling a story about a plant, bird, tree or garden an excellent device for quickening a child's curiosity. Even better, if a child hears a story about a plant as they are seeing, touching and sniffing it, they usually remember that plant. The livelier and more exciting the story, the greater the interest in the plant and the stronger the memory. Stories about garden and woodland fairies, the plants they live in and the adventures they have, are very exciting! Children don't forget them.

Literature is rich with wonderful stories involving plants, gardens and nature. Do the stories have to be absolutely true? Not necessarily. Fictional or factual, a story should capture a child's attention and stir their curiosity about the natural world they are part of. Myths, folktales and fairytales all contain elements of factual information that have become encrusted with fanciful details as the stories were passed through the centuries. Children love them.

Do parents and teachers have to tell children that myths and fairy stories are factual? Absolutely not. All the storyteller has to say is: " Did you know that once upon a time people believed that.....?". The child's imagination and level of maturity will be the guide from that point. When an older child looks the storyteller in the eye and asks " Do you believe that?" , the teller can honestly respond: "I've never been sure. What do you think?". After all, who is *really* sure when it comes to myths and fairytales? All we actually know is the stories are old, still being told and wonderful to hear!

A group of energetic first graders came to visit my garden on a perfect June afternoon. They wiggled and jiggled in place while introductions were being made and refreshments passed. They munched flower shaped cookies and drank fairy punch (mint, lemon balm and woodruff-infused raspberry ginger ale) served from a flower-decorated punch bowl.

Then the garden tour began. We went looking for plants the fairies might like and for plants that smelled good. The teachers and I showed the children how to touch leaves and flowers gently and warned them to be very careful not to step on any plants. After all, you wouldn't want to damage a fairy or elf that happened to be resting under a favorite leaf or in a flower. The children understood.

We visited the cowslips (*Primula veris*) and put our ears to the dangling clusters of golden bells to see if we could hear the fairies singing. We looked for the fairy rubies inside each bell. We found clumps of heartsease (*Viola tricolor*) and wondered at the little faces. The children learned all the different names for *Viola tricolor* and the stories of each name. They even tasted the flowers and leaves.

They obediently closed their eyes tight as I handed each child an Agastache leaf. With eyes squeezed shut, they rubbed and sniffed. "What does it smell like?" I asked. "Root beer", they shouted. We did the same

thing with peppermint. This time the answers were "Candy!"
"Toothpaste!" The tour continued. We touched, sniffed and nibbled our
way through the garden for over an hour. We had a wonderful time.

That was years ago. Every so often I see one of those kids, now in their
twenties. They usually say hello and then remind me of that long ago visit
when they were little. Did that experience have a profound effect on any of
them? I don't know. What I do know is the young adults I occasionally
meet still remember that day-- the stories, the garden, the fragrances--
and that is a good thing.

" If you want your children to be intelligent, read them fairy tales. If you want them to be more intelligent, read them more fairy tales.

When I examine myself and my methods of thought, I come to the conclusion that the gift of fantasy has meant more to me than any talent for abstract, positive thinking."

Albert Einstein (1879-1955)

CHAPTER TWO

What are Fairies? Where do they come from?

Plants are so vital to the physical survival and psychological well-being of the human race that it isn't hard to understand how, from the very beginning of human history, most people believed that every plant was home to a living spirit or protected by a god or goddess. Many of our most common superstitions come from those early beliefs. Have you ever knocked on wood for luck? A long-ago woodsmen would never cut down a tree without first knocking on it's trunk to alert the tree's spirit. If a tree was attacked without warning, its angered spirit could cause the tree to crush the attacker. Many newly framed buildings are still topped off with an evergreen tree or freshly cut evergreen branch, an ancient supplication to the god of woods and forests to bless the building and those who dwell there.

Almost every culture in the world has an oral or written tradition of fairy-like beings whose magical, enchanted lives parallel those of ordinary mortals. No matter how different cultures appear on the surface, their enchantment tales and plant lore customs have surprisingly similar profiles.

Written references to fairies date back at least to the time of Chaucer (1340-1400), who wrote that in "ancient times" fairies danced on village greens but that in his "modern times" they were no longer seen.

Shakespeare made similar references to the "once-upon-a-time-ness" of fairies, as did many of the English poets and writers who followed. Who are these mysterious creatures from long ago who didn't ever exist in the present but always did in the past?

There are several theories about the origin of our fairy traditions. One suggests that fairies are shadowy memories of ancient nature spirits, a folk memory of a time when people believed every living thing contained a spirit deserving recognition and respect. Another proposes that stories of a magical populace that peopled the dark hours of night were actually a memory of ancient displaced or conquered peoples who, driven to the outer limits of civilization, created a subculture that flourished from dusk to dawn while the victorious invaders slept. A third idea places fairies in the ghost category and suggests stories about fairies developed from the ancient belief that some spirits can live on after the body dies. Many folklorists feel myths, fairy and folktales grew out of early human attempts to explain the world around them. At the core of most familiar stories lie ancient observations on the workings of nature and our human place within the natural system. Some scholars have pointed out that the majority of these are cautionary tales. If humans follow the mythical peoples' code of ethics toward life and nature, then all will be well. If we do not, disaster will surely fall. Finally, there is the argument that a blending of all these theories is closest to the truth: fairies are part nature spirit, part ghost, part memory of forgotten races, and part the creation of observant early humans attempting to make sense of natural phenomena.

Maybe it doesn't really matter what fairies are and where they came from. Perhaps what is truly important is that we neither forget our cultural traditions nor downplay their importance in our lives or in the lives of all the people who preceded us. Cultural traditions tie us firmly to both the near and distant past. At the heart of our oldest folk and fairy tales, seasonal customs and traditional songs lie truths about life and how to live it well. Those truths are as valid today as they were thousands of years ago. Our old stories and traditions are encoded gifts from our ancestors, perhaps even from the fairies.

CHAPTER THREE

The Victorians and the Fairies

Today's stories about fairies are remnants, distillations and variations of ancient stories passed down through centuries of retelling. They were collected, categorized and recorded during the nineteenth century, primarily by the intellectually curious and energetic Victorians (c.1840-1900).

Enthusiastic gardeners and naturalists, the Victorians were fascinated with nature both as a science and source of enchantment. Men and women from all walks of life studied botany, horticulture, astronomy, zoology, geology and folklore. During the Victorian age departments of folklore, designed to apply rigorous academic principles to the subject, were created in universities all over Europe and the British Isles. On the local level, groups of amateur folklorists formed clubs and societies whose mission was to collect and document the folk customs and tales of their area.

The Grimm brothers (1785-1863) in Germany, Hans Christian Andersen (1805-1875) in Denmark and Andrew Lang (1844-1912) in Scotland, were all leaders in the field of collecting and popularizing folk and fairy tales. In

1884, an Englishman, the Reverend Hilderic Friend (1852-1940) published *Flowers and Flower Lore,* an extraordinary compilation of plant and fairy trivia. At the same time Henry N. Ellacombe (1822-1916), an accomplished gardener and village vicar, mined the works of Shakespeare for all references to plants and fairies in his book, *Plantlore and Garden Craft of Shakespeare.*

Widespread interest in recording old beliefs and customs, coupled with an insatiable public desire to collect, categorize and display anything and everything, resulted in the publication of a significant body of folk and plant lore. Many of the books and articles were academic studies, but a few authors used the collected lore to write stories for children to enjoy. Beautifully illustrated books of poems, stories and songs celebrating nature, magic, heroes and fairy folk began to appear. The Land of Faërie, the mythical land of enchantment, and the very real world of garden and woodland were combined and explored in the charming pages of Victorian children's books. This unique Victorian blending of science and folklore, fact and fiction continued into the first half of the next century.

In the early part of the twentieth century, three young women, living in three different countries, independently began writing and illustrating picture books for children using woodland and garden fairies as a central theme.

Elsa Beskow, a Swedish art student, sold her first story about a brownie to a children's literary magazine in 1894, when she was just twenty. Married three years later, she continued writing and illustrating books for young children throughout her long life. Generations of Swedish children have grown up reading her stories about adventurous children and their exciting experiences. Her most beloved books, *Peter in Blueberry Land,* *Children of the Forest,* and *Woody, Hazel and Little Pip,* are all stories about fairies and nature. The books are as enchanting to today's children as they were to children over 100 years ago.

In Germany, Sibylle von Olfers, a beautiful young noblewoman in her early twenties, began writing and illustrating books for very young children. Her first book, *Snowflake Children,* the story of the snow fairies, was published in 1905. An instant favorite, it was followed by The *Story of the Root Children* in 1906. It too was immediately successful and has remained a beloved book ever since. For more then 100 years, *The Story of the Root Children* has taught 2 to 6 year olds about the cycle of the growing season and the ways of the fairies who dance through it.

In 1923, a gentle young Englishwoman, Cicely Mary Barker, published *Flower Fairies of the Spring*, the first of a series of pocket-sized books about plants and the fairies that live with them. True to her Victorian upbringing, Miss Barker's books not only taught children about the growth habits and life cycle of common plants through verses that accompanied each botanically correct illustration, but also introduced them to the imaginative world of fairies. Her books have been credited with teaching botany and horticulture to generations of British school children in a delightful and palatable way. Her work has never gone out of print, nor has its popularity and usefulness ever faded.

The children's books created by these three women, all products of the Victorian Age, still have the power to enchant and teach our modern high-tech children. In each fanciful tale, the element of truth that children understand is the world of nature and how it works. True magic is quietly waiting in the pages of these books, ready to beckon children away from virtual worlds and lead them to the real green and growing world outdoors.

CHAPTER FOUR

Lifestyle of Garden and Woodland Fairies

Fairies come in all sizes, shapes and colors. Folklorist Dr. Katherine Briggs includes almost every kind of mythical, other-worldly beings in her definitive work, *The Encyclopedia of Fairies*. According to her research bogeymen and leprechauns, brownies and elves, trolls and gnomes, mermaids and mermen, giants and banshees are all fairies, citizens of the land of Faërie.

By most traditional accounts, life in the country of Faërie closely parallels the human world. Some of its citizens are good, some evil, and some a bit of both. Most residents of Faërie live in groups, clans and families. There are nuclear families and extended ones. There are solitary fairies, who prefer to live totally alone, while others thrive in large, sometimes boisterous groups. Some fairies live in a single spot for a thousand years, a few forever roam the earth, never settling down. Many of the citizens of Faërie prefer not to interact with humans, so are rarely seen. Down through the centuries, the group most widely reported to have periodic contact with humans are the nature fairies, the ones we call by the name of their land, Faërie.

The tiny, quick-moving sprites most people call fairies are part of the nature fairy group. They are garden and woodland fairies who belong to the clan called "Trooping Fairies." Trooping fairies are by far the most numerous type of fairy. They live together in large, gregarious groups, generally wear green clothes and love to sing and dance.

According to traditional stories, garden and woodland fairies have a government headed by a king and queen who are attended by courtiers, knights, ladies-in-waiting and soldiers. The ordinary citizens of the woodland and garden fairy clan are often reported to be highly skilled craftsmen: spinners and weavers, metalsmithes and shoemakers, tailors and bakers, midwives and homemakers. They can marry and have children. They generally have extremely long lives, but occasionally one dies and a funeral is held.

Closely tied to the cycle of the seasons, the fairies of the woods and garden slumber through the cold winter and awaken in the spring as the earth warms. They are very active throughout the growing season, then tuck themselves back in for a long nap as winter approaches. It's the woodland and garden fairies who create fairy rings. The fairies of the wood and forest dance on circular patches of moss and lichens growing in sunlit clearings or where paths cross. Garden fairies prefer circles of mushrooms in the grass or rounded areas of tiny flowers or thyme at the edge of a garden for their dancing spots. *A traditional word of warning to those who find a fairy ring: Do not step in it! Always walk around it. Humans who step in fairy rings can be carried off to fairyland, never to be seen again.*

The homes of ordinary fairy folk tend to be simple. Garden fairies live in their flowers or mounds of fragrant green thyme. Woodland fairies usually prefer the trees, shrubs, mosses and ferns of their woods or forest. Some stories tell of fairy huts built by the side of remote country lanes or deep in the heart of dense woods.

The fairy king and queen and all their court live quite differently. They are said to live in a golden castle covered with sparkling gems which floats lightly on the air. Some stories report the royal fairy castle is hidden hidden deep inside a hollow hill, others claim it is located on a wild, secluded mountain top.

CHAPTER FIVE

Rules of Fairy Etiquette or how to Interact with Fairies

Most fairies avoid humans. They generally view us as a noisy, smelly and destructive race, lacking in values and ethics. They will interact with humans if absolutely necessary but prefer to keep their distance. Sometimes a fairy will notice a human so kind and virtuous that they feel a reward is in order or one so totally reprehensible that a severe punishment is needed. However, fairy and mortal do occasionally meet unexpectedly. Should that occur, it is very important to know the traditional code of fairy etiquette. Fairies are easily offended by human behavior and can be very vindictive. They believe humans cannot claim ignorance of fairy ways since we should instinctively know the ancient rules of good manners and fair dealing.

- First and foremost, fairies do not like to be called "fairies". They prefer to be referred to as "the Folk," "the Gentry," "the People of Peace," "the Little Folk" or "the Good Neighbors." This is a hard rule for humans to follow, since most of us have used the term "fairies" all our lives. Do try though, especially if you happen to meet one of the good folk somewhere and need to speak to them. An old Scottish rhyme warns:

"...if you call me a fairy,
I'll work you very hard;
If good neighbor you call me
Then good neighbor I'll be."

- The good folk value their privacy. They strongly resent being studied or spied upon. They believe their business is their own and none other's. Never stare if you happen upon one of them. Look quickly away, murmur a polite "Good day, neighbor" and leave as quietly as you can.

- Don't ever be tempted to steal from the good folk. Many rash, greedy humans have tried, but few have ever been successful. Almost all have been caught and sternly punished.

- The little people are neat and tidy by nature and they respect those qualities in mortals. Many a slovenly housekeeper or lazy farmer has awakened in the morning with unexplained black and blue marks on their bodies. A sharp pinch during the night is the little peoples' first warning that behavior needs improving.

- Fairies are hard working and thrifty. It pleases them to see humans practice those virtues.

- The little people note with approval when a human is kind, with no thought of personal gain. On rare occasions, they have been known to reward such good behavior.

- The fairies expect total honesty at all times. One cannot ever equivocate with a fairy!

Should a fairy find a human who combines all these qualities with an open, loving nature and joy of living, then it is possible for a friendship to develop. According to tradition if you befriend a fairy you may find little homely tasks being done to perfection by unseen hands. Beds may be made, dishes washed, gardens weeded or babies rocked. A family business may prosper and loving relationships deepen.

A human who recognizes acts of friendship from the little people will naturally want to reciprocate. After all, it is our custom to say "thank you" for gifts and kindnesses and, if we are especially grateful, even give a gift in return. Don't do it. This is not the custom of the little people and will only offend them, perhaps even drive them away. Fairies will graciously accept spoken appreciation but not "thank you." For example, if you find the table unexpectedly set for dinner say " How lovely, what a beautiful table." instead of "Thank you, dear neighbor". If you must give a present to a fairy friend, there are three traditional gifts a human adult can give without serious offense: a bowl of fresh milk or cream, a slice of good bread or a piece of well aged cheese. All fairies love and appreciate these things.

A child who befriends a fairy has more leeway in gift giving. All presents given with love by a child seem to be acceptable to the little people. However, it has been noticed that they are especially fond of gifts that come from nature. A lovely flower, a soft bird's feather, a beautiful twist of bark or a special stone, presented by a child as a gift to a fairy friend, are all warmly received.

CHAPTER SIX

Fairy celebrations

Like humans, the little people have special days set aside each year for
celebration and feasting. Traditionally, the fairies' high festival days are
May Eve, the evening of April 30; Midsummer's Night Eve, the evening of
the summer solstice, somewhere between June 21 and June 25 and All
Hallows Eve or Halloween, October 31. Stories say the fairies gather for
exuberant revels on each feast day. Groups sing and dance until dawn in
woods and gardens. Merry-making little people dance wildly across
meadows, through fields and down the streets of towns, sometimes
careening through human homes and releasing farm animals from pens.
It was believed that on these three special nights the barrier separating
the world of Faërie from the human world thinned, allowing members of
both races to pass through it freely.

May Eve was a joyful night for the fairies. Newly awakened from their
long winter sleep, the little people were said to be bursting with energy,
ready to celebrate their return to the woods and garden. In parts of
Europe and the British Isles bonfires burned all night to prevent the
fairies from reveling through farms and villages. Prudent humans hung
bunches of primroses or branches of flowering hawthorn on doors and
windows to protect their property from the merry makers. Today, some
families still follow the delightful May Eve custom of leaving a plate of
tiny cakes in the garden for the happy fairies to decorate as they dance
through.

Midsummer's Night Eve, as Shakespeare pointed out, is a night of high fairy mischief and magic. Bonfires once again blazed on hilltops. Humans who preferred not to have celebrating fairies racing through their property would decorate doors and gateways with bunches of fennel and mugwort, herbs powerful enough to keep most fairies away.

Many stories say that exactly at midnight on Midsummer's Night Eve, the fairy king and his entire court ride through the countryside, resplendent on their dainty fairy horses. A curious mortal who wished to watch the spectacle had to prepare very carefully. Spying on fairies can be a risky business. If detected, a person could be carried off to fairyland, never to be seen again. First, a human should eat no meat for at least one 24 hours before the Ride. Fairies eat only fruits, vegetables. grains and nuts. They can smell a meat-eater from far away. Secondly, the person must bathe thoroughly, then dress in clean clothes. Finally, at the stroke of midnight on Midsummer's Night Eve, the person must stand in total silence by the trunk of an elder tree, a traditional home of the queen of the fairies, not moving until the cavalcade has passed by.

On the ancient Celtic calendar, All Hallows Eve, October 31st, was a day that floated between the end of the Celtic old year, October 30th, and the beginning of the Celtic new year, November l st. During this twenty four hour period, many people believed all the laws of nature were in suspension and the veil that separated the human world from the fairy world was gone. Fairy mounds, underground dwellings of Celtic fairies, would burst open and all the fairies would come dancing out for a last round of merry-making before their long winter sleep. This was the one night of the year that humans who had been abducted by fairies could escape and find their way home. Once again, bonfires lit up hilltops in an

effort to keep the little people and other wandering spirits at bay. However, at this time people would hang sprays of grain on their doors and leave out other food and drink so the wandering spirits could refresh themselves as the night wore on, the old year ended and the garden and woodland fairies settled down for the winter.

CHAPTER SEVEN

The Fairies Favorite Plants

When the winds of March are wakening the crocuses and crickets,
Did you ever find a fairy near some budding little thickets,...
And when she sees you creeping up to get a closer peek
She tumbles through the daffodils, a playing hide and seek.
~Marjorie Barrows

Down through the centuries, stories and legends about fairies from Europe and the British Isles have repeatedly mentioned certain plants favored or used by the little people. Many of the plants widely associated with fairies are old and respected medicinal herbs. Others grow naturally in the wild places fairies were thought to live. Use these plants to grow a fairy garden. It's fun and, just maybe, the fairies *will* come to live there. You never know with the little people!

Flowers and Herbs

Blue Flax (_Linum perrene_) The lovely little blue-eyed flax is often called fairy flax. It is said the fairies grew it to spin the thread they wove into delicate linens. If you look closely at the grass early on a dewy summer morning, you might see those freshly laundered linens spread out to dry.

Cowslips (_Primula veris_) The lovely yellow wild primroses of April and May are special favorites of the fairies. Children called the individual blossoms golden fairy cups. The little red dots on the inside of the cups were fairy rubies.

The hanging cluster of yellow bells on the top of the cowslips' slender green stalk was said to turn into the keys to fairyland if picked by a person favored by the little people. A human befriended by a fairy and given the keys to fairyland was always treated with kindness and generosity, unless the human visitor tried to trick the fairies. If that happened punishment was swift and severe, the friendship lost forever.

On rainy days, stories told, fairies nestled inside the dangling golden cowslip flowers to stay dry. Sometimes the resting fairies sang. If a person, passing a stand of cowslips on a drizzly day, bent quietly down and put their ear to a cowslip bell, they could often hear the sweet music made by fairy voices.

Ferns (Osmunda) Discreetly placed ferns offer the fairies a privacy screen if grown near the moss or thyme beds that fairies so often frequent.

Forget me not (Myosotis) Legends say that when held in the hand of a pure hearted person, the little sky blue flowers of forget me not turn into the keys to all the treasure rooms of fairyland.

Foxgloves (Digitalis purpurea) Associated with fairies all across northern Europe and the British Isles, wild foxglove has many old names: Fairy caps, Fairy gloves, Fairy bells, Fairy petticoats, Fairy fingers and Fairy thimbles. Some stories said that a flourishing stand of foxglove marked the entrance to a fairy's home.

A respected medicinal herb, the tall spires of foxglove are a delight in any garden, however, foxglove is toxic and should never be eaten.

Heartsease (_Viola tricolor_) The original wild pansy, heartsease has many old names: Three-faces-in-a-hood, Love-in-idleness, Ladies' delight, Johnny-jump-up and Cupid's flower.

In Shakespeare's _A Midsummer Night's Dream_, Cupid's flower _(Viola tricolor)_ was used by Puck as a magic love potion. The king and queen of the fairies were having an argument. Directed by Oberon, the king, to find a way to punish his wife Titania for not obeying him, Puck squeezed a drop of juice from a little heartease flower onto the eyelids of the sleeping fairy queen. When she awoke, she fell hopelessly in love with the first living creature she saw, a donkey!

Hollyhocks (_Alcea rosea)_ Children used to call the flat, round seed cases of hollyhock fairy cheeses because they look like tiny old fashioned wheels of cheese.

Lily of the valley (_Convallaria majalis)_ Often called fairy caps or fairy bells, lily of the valley is the flower of May, symbol of the return of happiness. Its sweetly scented white flowers are said to ring whenever the fairies sing.

Historically considered an effective medicinal herb, all parts of the plant are toxic, especially the leaves and red berries that appear in autumn.

Monkshood (_Aconitum napellus_) The purplish-blue hat shaped flowers of wild monkshood were often called fairy helmets. Folklore said they were worn by knights in the fairy king's court as well as by the palace guards.

Often called wolfbane, monkshood is a very poisonous plant and shouldn't be grown in a child's garden.

Moss (Bryophytes) The good folk are fond of velvety green moss. If you have a secluded, mossy patch or can establish one in your garden or woods, you may be rewarded by fairy revelry on summer nights.

Narcissus (*Narcissus tazetta*) There is a story that says the fragrant bulb flower we call Paper White was a gift to the Chinese people from the water fairies. It is grown in homes during the Asian New Year celebration to bring the family luck in the coming year.

Rosemary (*Rosmarinus officinalis*) In Sicily rosemary can become a very large shrub. Legends say fairies make their homes under rosemarys and rock their babies in the plant's tiny blue flowers. Rosemary was also especially loved by the fairies in Portugal and often called Elfin plant.

St. Johnswort (*Hypericum perforatum*) St. Johnswort was named for St. John the Baptist, whose feast day, June 24, is part of traditional Midsummer celebrations. An important medicinal herb, it was also believed to have strong magical powers. Some stories said St. Johnswort was the daytime guise of fairy horses and warned people to beware. Should a mortal step on a stem of St. Johnswort just as the sun was setting it could turn into a fairy horse and carry him away, especially during Midsummer!

Thyme (*Thymus vulgaris*) Thyme is the fairies very favorite plant. They love its color, smell and bounciness. The little people will gather on all thyme plants, but creeping mother-of -thyme (*Thymus serpyllum)* is their preferred variety. Busy fairy folk use thyme as a resting place during the day and a dance floor at night. Fairy babies are tucked into fragrant green beds of thyme.

A mound of mother-of-thyme growing in a meadow or near the edge of a garden is a fairy ring, used on summer nights for dances and other community gatherings.

Tulips *(Tulipia)* Tulips are used by the fairies as springtime cradles to gently rock their babies to sleep while the adults are dancing nearby.

Trees

Apple (*Pyrus malus*) The apple tree figures strongly in ancient Celtic mythology. They believed it was a tree of enchantment, inhabited by the fairies. Mortals who lingered too long under an apple tree might find themselves whisked away to fairyland.

As King Arthur lay dying on the battlefield, Morgan Le Fay and her ladies-in-waiting gathered him up, laid him gently in a boat and ferried him to Avalon, island of apples and ancestral home of the fairies.

Legend says he still lives on the Isle of Avalon with the fairies, waiting for a time of great need to return to his kingdom.

Black Elder (*Sambucus nigra*) Northern European legends say Hulda, Queen of the Fairies, lives under the roots of the elder tree. Tradition says the tree must never be cut, nor its fruits and flowers picked, without first asking her permission.

If you sit with quiet respect under an elder tree exactly at midnight on Midsummer's Eve, you will see the King of the Fairies and all his court parade proudly by.

Hawthorn (_Crataegus monogyna)_ The abundant white flowers of hawthorn were the original Mayflower. When the thorny, twisted branches of hawthorn trees and hedgerows burst into full bloom sometime in May, people knew winter was over and summer was coming. Ancient stories from all over Europe and the British Isles associate hawthorn with gods, goddesses and fairies.

In Ireland the fairies are believed to live in and around hawthorn trees to this very day, especially those that grow in groups of three or stand alone in meadows or on hilltops. A prudent farmer, who has a hawthorn growing in a field, always carefully plows around it. Woe to the mortal who damages or destroys a hawthorn tree, for he shall suffer a lifetime of bad fortune!

It is considered bad luck to bring bunches of hawthorn flowers indoors. However, on May Eve doorways and gates can be decorated with them to discourage frolicking fairies from dancing through the house. The round red berries that cover thorn trees in the fall are often called "Pixie Apples."

Oak tree (_Quercus)_ An old saying warns, "Fairy folks live in old oaks." Once upon a time people were cautioned to speak softly and kindly when passing an old oak tree. Children were sternly reminded to be on their best behavior. It was widely believed that holes in the trunks of old oaks were doorways that led straight to the land of Faerie. Any poor behavior on the part of mortals near the oaks would be loudly broadcast over the land of enchantment, possibly resulting in angry reactions from the disturbed little people.

Many references to specific plants and fairies are found throughout European literature. Two especially charming ones come from Elizabethan England.

In Shakespeare's *"A Midsummer Night's Dream"* Titania, Queen of the Fairies, slept in a bank of nodding violets and wild thyme under a canopy of fragrant eglantine, musk rose and sweetly scented woodbine (honeysuckle). Another poet, Michael Drayton described a fairy wedding. The bride, dressed all in green, wore a gown made of "pansy, pink and primrose leaves." Her bridal bed was of roses, the bed curtains and tester sewn from Crown Imperial petals. The fringe of the bed curtains were hung with blue harebell blossoms, and the pillows were made from lilies stuffed with butterfly down. What an enchanting sight that must have been!

CHAPTER EIGHT

The Fairy Festival

Spring in New England is a chancy thing, some years we have it, some years we don't. It's supposed to come in May but sometimes arrives in April, almost never appears in March, and occasionally waits until June. We are quite used to snow covered ground on March 21st, the first day of spring. Easter, the traditional spring celebration, slides up and down the calendar between March 21st and April 25th. It often arrives without a flower or tender new leaf in sight. It's hard to celebrate spring in New England, which is one reason I decided to hold a festival for the fairies.

The idea of a fairy festival is based on the Celtic tradition that the little people awakened from their winter sleep and returned to the woods and gardens on May Eve, bringing exuberant new growth to the plant world. A fairy festival is a spring play day that allows children and adults to share the sheer joy of being outdoors, reveling in the return of the growing season. It's a good, old fashioned celebration of the return of fragrance and leafy green beauty to the landscape.

I held the first Faerie Festival in 1988. At that time I owned an herb and garden shop. We had our own line of dried flower wreaths and arrangements as well as herb plants, books, fragrances, potpourri and garden accessories. I wanted to find a unique way to celebrate spring in the shop. I also wanted to remind our customers of some seasonal traditions that seemed to be vanishing. We already had a national reputation for our signature dried flower wreath called a "Fairy Ring"(tm) as well as the little moss baskets we made. It was a short step to promoting the beginning of New England's growing season by celebrating the traditional return of fairies to gardens and woods.

Planning for the first festival began in February. We planned to have the festival on Saturday, April 30, May Eve. We ran into a problem almost immediately. Our neighboring shops had reservations about the name of the festival. In the late nineteenth century, the lovely ancient word "faerie" had begun to acquire negative connotations. By the end of the 1980s, "fairy" was rarely used in reference to the mythical little people of woodland and garden. It had become a slur. To answer our neighbors' concerns, I wrote an information sheet explaining who and what fairies were and how they were connected to spring, horticulture and ecology. My husband illustrated it with pictures of garden fairies. We printed several hundred copies and distributed them to all the shops in our neighborhood. The shop owners understood and handed them out to interested customers. Plans for the festival continued.

The first Faerie Festival was small, local, and very informal. We asked friends and customers who enjoyed singing, played an instrument, told stories or loved to read aloud if they would like to participate. A staff member offered to make fairy cakes and meringue mushrooms for all attendees. We devised a recipe for magical fairy punch.

The day before the Faerie Festival, my staff and I cut armloads of golden forsythia and newly leafed branches. We stood them in tubs and containers full of water, inside and outside of the shop. Early on the morning of the festival, we tied streamers of brightly colored ribbons everywhere we could and set up a jerry-rigged canopy in our little cramped parking lot. We spread old rugs on the macadam and put out a few pillows and chairs. At 10 o'clock, we rang bells to signal the opening of the festival. Everyone who came was offered a flower, a tiny fairy cake and a little glass of fairy punch. We sang, listened to stories, wove flower crowns and built fairy houses from leaves and twigs. People of all ages played happily together. We had a wonderful time!

WOULD YOU CARE FOR A FAIRY CAKE?

I didn't know it then, but we may have been reviving what was once a tradition in early France. A book about fairy mythology, written in 1828, describes a celebration held in May each year to honor a fairy named Melusine. Since at least the 13th century, the festival had been held in a meadow near a fountain called "The Fountain of the Fairies." The special food of the day was a small cake or cookie in the shape of the fairy, half woman and half serpent!

Today there are herb farms, shops, libraries, schools, botanical gardens and arboretums throughout the country that hold fairy festivals. Some schools teach beginning horticulture and plant science by having students design and grow fairy gardens. Fairy festivals have also been used by some elementary schools as a closing event to a unit combining reading, math, music, art and science skills with practice in cooperation and good citizenship.

CHAPTER NINE

Planning a Fairy Festival

Fairy festivals fall into two categories, a public event or personal play day with family and friends. A fairy festival open to the public could be a special promotion for a shop or garden center to attract and educate customers or can be used as a fund raiser for a public garden or other institution. A private fairy festival is simply a party celebrating the beauty of nature and the sheer joy of spending a day outdoors with people you like being with.

A Personal Fairy Day

A fairy play day is fun to plan. Pick a day near May Day if you can, but any day will do. Choose a location you enjoy being in. It could be your backyard, a public park, a beach or any accessible natural area. Private estates that have become museums are often excellent places to hold a fairy picnic. The lovely old houses usually have spacious grounds planted with groves of very old trees and tangled, mossy areas hidden from view. They are perfect spots to catch a glimpse of a fairy.

Invite family and friends of all ages. Be sure to tell your guests this will be a whimsical day spent outdoors. If the Fairy Day is not in your backyard, advise them to dress in comfortable, sit-upon-the-ground clothes and be prepared for a little walk.

Create a picnic menu featuring foods the little people might enjoy: fruits, vegetables, grains, cheeses and nuts. Make a portable fairy punch for the children and include a little May wine for adults who might like a sip. Don't forget the fairy cakes.

fairy Cakes and May Wine

Plan a project or two for your group, such as building tiny fairy houses at the base of trees using twigs, leaves and mosses you find on the ground. Ask each guest to bring a favorite poem or story about fairies, gardens, plants or nature to read aloud. Borrow some of the Cicely Mary Barker *Flower Fairy* books from the library. Can you identify any plants or trees using the pictures and verses in her books?

Spread a blanket on the grass. Lie on your back and look up at the sky. What shapes do you see? Close your eyes and listen to the natural sounds around you. Be aware of the fragrances of the earth. At the end of the day comment out loud how much you enjoyed yourself. The little people like that!

Public Fairy Festivals

A public Faerie Festival takes more planning and organizing but is essentially the same as a private one -- a play day for adults and children emphasizing the return of the growing season, its stories, flavors, sounds and fragrances.

Begin your planning six to nine months in advance of the festival. Do the practical things first. Choose your date, then check with public officials. Do you need any special permits to hold a public event. Are you required to hire policemen to direct traffic? Where will people park? Do you need tents? Where will they go? What about bathrooms for expected attendees? Should you rent some? Is a temporary liability policy needed for the duration of the event? Who is responsible for trash clean-up and disposal?

Once those things are settled, begin inviting entertainers, speakers and teachers. Contact storytellers, musicians, actors groups and street entertainers. Invite speakers who will educate, as well as entertain, your attendees. Find teachers for fairy related classes. When you have confirmed who your speakers and performers will be, draw up a schedule. Be sure there is something interesting happening all the time. For example, schedule musicians to play in one area while a talk on planting a fairy garden is going on somewhere else or ask jugglers and magicians to wander through the crowd while a storyteller enchants children in a quite spot.

Offer classes in building fairy houses, decorating fairy furniture, and making fairy baskets that adults and children can attend together. Plan an exhibit on fairy plants with cultural directions and suggestions on creating fairy gardens. Arrange for enough tiny fairy cakes and fairy punch so everyone attending can have a taste.

Assign someone to be in charge of passing the cakes and pouring the punch. One taste of magic per person is just fine.

In press releases and advertising, encourage people to come dressed as fairies. If some people do come in costume be sure to have a fairy parade. Ask the musicians and street entertainers to lead it.

Create a fairy marketplace. Advertise for craftspeople and artists who specialize in fairy-oriented products. Rent them selling space for the length of the festival. Be sure to include a food vendor. People of all ages like to eat!

Finally, be sure there is a generous supply of fairy dust available for sprinkling, so the day never loses its magic!

CHAPTER TEN

Fairy Festival Recipes

Fairy cakes are an English tradition. Although made by human hands, the fairies decorate them. Just before bedtime on May Eve, take a plateful of tiny undecorated cakes to the garden. Leave them in a spot you think the fairies might favor. With luck, in the morning you will discover they have been beautifully decorated. Who did it? Why, the fairies, of course!

Fairy Cakes

3 large eggs at room temperature
1 cup sugar
5 tablespoons milk
1 teaspoon pure vanilla extract
1 cup flour
1 teaspoon baking powder
¼ teaspoon salt

Preheat oven to 375* F. Butter and flour a 12 ½ inch by 10 ½ inch jellyroll pan.

In a bowl, beat eggs until thick and fluffy. Gradually add the sugar, beating well after each addition. Beat in milk and vanilla extract. Mix together flour, baking powder and salt. Add dry ingredients to egg mixture and beat until smooth. Spread the batter in the pan.Bake for l2 to 15 minutes. When cool, cut into circles with a tiny biscuit cutter or into small squares.

Decorate each little cake with unsprayed edible flowers such as violets and heartsease. Tiny mint leaves are delicious also. Attach the flowers and leaves with a dab of the following frosting.

Frosting Flowers for Fairy Cakes

You will need 4 small bowls and 4 pastry bags, each with a different tip. Use one bag for each color frosting.

> *1/2 cup butter, at room temperature*
> *1/2 to 3/4 cup powdered sugar*
> *3/4 teaspoon strawberry or vanilla extract*
> *1 to 3 teaspoons milk or cream*
> *Blue, red, green and yellow food coloring*

Beat butter and sugar together. Add the extract and enough milk or cream to give the frosting a good spreading texture. Divide the frosting into the 4 bowls. Add one drop of blue to first bowl; one drop of red to second bowl; one drop of green to third bowl; and one drop of yellow to fourth bowl. Mix well. Fill each bag with one color. Decorate the fairy cakes with leaves and flowers. Have fun!

(The fairy cake and frosting recipes were developed by Victoria Anderson, master fairy cake baker and decorator.)

Floral Ice Ring

It is easy to make an ice ring. You will need a circular mold such as those used for gelatin salads and aspics. Fill the mold about one quarter full with water. Carefully place it in your freezer. Be sure it lays flat in the freezer so that it layers evenly.

While it is freezing, go to your garden and gather a collection of the little peoples' favorite herbs and flowers: sprigs of thymes, violet flowers, small unblemished violet leaves, strawberry flowers, small perfect strawberry leaves, whorls of woodruff and woodruff flowers, heartease, viola and pansy flowers.

When the water has frozen, remove the mold from the freezer. Lightly sprinkle the shallow ice ring with leaves and flowers. Add enough water to half-fill the mold and freeze again. When frozen, repeat the process one more time but don't quite fill the mold with water. Refreeze. When solidly frozen, fill the mold to the brim with water. Freeze again. You should end up with a thick ring of ice embedded with herbs and flowers. The reason for the gradual filling is to keep the flowers and leaves from floating to the surface of the ring during freezing.

When you are ready to use the ice ring, dip the mold briefly into hot water to loosen the ice. Slip the frozen ring into the punch bowl.

Faerie Punch

Faerie punch *should* be blended from the sweet drops of spring rain and early morning dew, flavored with the nectar of primroses and violets. However, we found it difficult to make enough to serve all the thirsty mortals who wished to sip it, so we headed for the grocery store and created the following secret recipe:

> *2 to 3 large bottles of raspberry ginger ale*
> *½ pint fresh strawberries*
> *Fresh picked woodruff leaves and flowers, heartsease flowers (Johnny-jump-ups), mint sprigs, violets and violet leaves*

Chill the ginger ale and pour into the most beautiful glass punch bowl you can find. Slice the strawberries into the ginger ale. Add ice cubes or decorate with a frozen floral ice ring Sprinkle heartsease, violet flowers and woodruff sprigs onto the surface of the punch.

There is no lovelier presentation for a bowl of Fairy Punch or May Wine than a woodsy garden scene around the base of the bowl. Bank the punch bowl with little pots of lushly grown sweet woodruff, alpine strawberries, thyme and blooming heartsease or violas. Camouflage the pots by tucking green moss, pieces of lichens and decorative bark around them. Finish your spring fantasy by floating a gorgeous floral ice ring on top of the wine instead of ordinary ice cubes. Serve the magical punch in small glass cups. Sip and dream.

May Bowl

If you are entertaining adult guests at your home for a May Day or Faerie party, the following is probably closer to a true Faerie punch. The fairies are not meek and mild creatures!

> *2 bottles Rhine wine*
> *½ cup freshly picked sweet woodruff leaves, ¼ cup per bottle*
> *½ pint brandy*
> *½ pint strawberries*

Open each bottle. Add ¼ cup woodruff leaves to each along with 3 to 4 sliced strawberries. Recap the bottles. Allow the wine to steep for 3 or 4 days. On the day of the party, chill the wine for several hours. Strain the infused wine into a glass punchbowl. Add 1/2 pint of brandy to the bowl. Stir.

Decorate with a floral ice ring.(See directions on page 48 for Floral Ice Ring.) Float whole strawberries, violets, heartsease flowers and sprigs of woodruff and woodruff flowers on the surface of the wine. Create a woodland or garden scene at the base of the bowl.

Serve in glass punch cups with a slice of strawberry and a flower in each one.

CHAPTER ELEVEN

Making Fairy Dust

No fairy play day is complete without fairy dust and lots of it!

Every child who has heard of fairies knows exactly what fairy dust is and how to use it. What isn't so well known is how to make it. Of course, the recipe for real fairy dust, or fairy glamour as it is often called, is known only to the little people. However, the following is a pretty close approximation that any ordinary human can stir up.

You will need:

5 to 6 quarts of dried herb and flower leaves and petals.
1 cup gold or silver glitter
1 large container for mixing

Pour the dried leaves and petals into the mixing container. Add the glitter. Mix gently but thoroughly. Mutter a few favorite magic words. Mix again. The fairy dust is now ready for sprinkling. Put it in a twiggy basket or other woodsy looking container. Decorate the container with colorful ribbons or swoops of tulle. Place the fairy dust where anyone who needs a pinch can easily take it.

Leaves and petals of garden and roadside herbs and flowers are very easy to dry. Almost any will dry and become crumbly, so don't feel restricted. If you are able to gather from your yard or the gardens of friends and neighbors, collect any small leaf or flower that is available. For example, in the early spring, forsythia's vibrant golden flowers stay bright yellow after they are dry. They are a colorful addition to a fairy dust collection, as are the flowers of other flowering shrubs and trees. Don't overlook the flowers and leaves of the weedy herbs growing in lawns and by the roadside: violets, dandelions, ajuga, gill-over-the-ground, Queen Ann's lace, goldenrod, fennel, loosestrife and many more. The fading flowers of spring bulbs are great additions to a fairy dust mix, as are the falling petals of poppies, roses and peonies.

Choose the hottest, driest place you have to dehydrate the leaves and petals. A single layer of plant material, spread thinly on a flat basket, cookie sheet or wire screen, will dry to a crisp state in 4 or 5 days if kept in a consistently warm spot of 80 degrees or higher. Some of the best places to dry plant material in the average home are: on top of the refrigerator, over the furnace, in the trunk of a car or back of a van, in a hot, dry attic or near a dehumidifier. If you are very watchful and can leave the door slightly ajar, single layers of plant material can be dried in an over set at 100 to 125 degrees. When the leaves and petals are totally crisp, store them in an insect and moisture-proof container until ready to use.

Another possible source of leaves and petals is a local florist. Florists regularly throw out old flowers. Contact local florist shops and ask if you can pick up discarded flowers for a week or two. If they agree, take them a special wastebasket to use just for your petal collection. Be sure to present them with a generous bag of fairy dust after it is made. Even florists need a little fairy magic sometimes!

If you can plan for a spring Faerie Festival during the preceding summer, two or three people collecting and drying a few leaves and flowers each day can rapidly build a good supply of fairy dust material.

CHAPTER TWELVE

Building Fairy Houses

Building fairy houses in the woods is a century-old tradition on some of the islands off the coast of Maine. This delightful custom is maintained by both natives and visitors. Each spring fairy houses appear in the pine forests of the islands. Constructed of bits of bark, flat stones, twigs and other forest floor findings, each little house is a unique and charming creation. No one ever sees the houses being built. They just appear and remain in secluded parts of the forest until the winter storms destroy them. In the spring new ones appear.

It is fun and easy to build fairy houses. They can be created in a peaceful spot in your garden, in a meadow, at the beach, in the woods, or even on your back porch.

Fran McCormick, a talented artist, teacher and appreciative observer of nature, introduced me to the fairy houses of Maine. She saw her first fairy house while walking through the pine woods on one of those Maine islands. She was so entranced that she took a series of photographs of the houses. After developing the pictures, she decided to create a book for them. First she made the paper for the book, then mounted the pictures and bound the pages together. I saw the book and became completely enraptured with the idea of celebrating spring with a festival of fairies and fairy houses.

Fran taught our fairy house classes every year. She generously wrote down her thoughts and ideas on fairy house construction beginning with this lyrical list:

"The directions are few,
The possibilities many,
The process engaging,
The results delightful!"

You will need a selection of natural materials that are native to your area. Use only bits of nature that have dropped or dried. Collect all sizes. As you gather and handle them, let the materials suggest possible uses to you.

Look for:

bark	*egg shells*	*pine needles*
twigs	*seed pods*	*grasses*
nut shells	*ferns*	*sea shells*
cones	*acorns*	*stones*
mosses & lichen	*fallen leaves*	*seaweed*

Choose a site. Some favorite locations are under a bush, in a hollow log, on top of a boulder, tucked against a piece of driftwood, in the roots of a tree, or at the back of the garden. Any place that is natural feeling and out of the way of human traffic will do. Remember, fairies prefer privacy and a natural environment.

If you are building a fairy house for your back porch or deck, use a sheet of heavy cardboard or thin wood. Wooden shakes or shingles work well. An old basket works well also. If you construct on wood or cardboard, you will need white glue.

on-site construction

1. Clear your chosen spot of any unwanted debris.

2. Look over your collection of building materials and select something to become the walls. Prop up a slab of bark or a flat piece of stone. Try different pieces and positions. Twigs can function as posts to hold up the roof or to support the walls.

3. A sheet of moss makes a fine roof as does a thin piece of bark. You can construct a roofing framework of twigs and then cover it with grasses, ferns and leaves.

4. Try to create a cozy, sheltered area: a cave-like room, lean-to, A-frame, tent or gazebo. Remember you are building to accommodate a resident whose size is somewhere between a large beetle and a small field mouse.

5. Once the house is done you can add landscaping touches. Lay a pebbled path or plant a pine cone hedge. Create fences, gates and trellises from twigs and dried flower stalks.

6. Build porches, decks and patios.

7. Create furniture to add to the fairies' comfort. Build a table from bark or flat stones. Use nut shells for dishes, seeds for food. A small curl of bark becomes a chair or tiny bed. Use moss as cushions, a bedspread or carpeting. Leaves can be tablecloths or rugs. Beach fairies love sleeping in a scallop shell bed with a rockweed mattress and sea lettuce spread!

Porch or Deck Construction

1. Use your piece of heavy cardboard or thin wood as the base of the house. If you can, leave room around it to allow for landscaping.

2. Use white glue to attach your walls to the base. Prop or hold them in place while the glue dries. You may need to provide permanent support by gluing flat stones or clumps of moss to the base of the walls and the board.

3. Proceed as with the on-site house.

4. Landscape with mosses, lichen, pebbles and stones. They will probably need to be glued into place. Twigs can be used as shrubs and trees.

5. If you use a basket as a base, fill it with styrofoam, dry floral foam or soil. White glue won't be needed in the construction. Use twigs and pieces of bark, pushed into the foam or soil to support the walls of the house.

Portable fairy houses can be carried from construction site to home. If not

used on a porch or deck, they can become a delightful centerpiece on a spring table or a whimsical addition to a plant collection. As with all dried, naturally colored pieces, it is best to keep your faerie house out of direct sunlight. The sun can bleach and over-dry the natural materials.

CHAPTER THIRTEEN

moss Twiggy Baskets

Twig-handled, moss-covered baskets are charming acknowledgments of the return of the growing season. Inexpensive and quickly made, use them as Easter baskets, to display a plant or flower arrangement and, lined with a pretty napkin, to hold finger foods at spring and summer gatherings.

The technique for making moss baskets is simple. The materials used are widely available and easily gathered. I use a basket called a "Chinese rice bowl", round, shallow baskets that come in sizes ranging from 4 to 14 inches across. They are widely available and inexpensive. You can also look for basket bargains at garage sales and flea markets. Even baskets with broken handles are usable. Cut off the broken handle and wire a new twig one on in its place. When covered with sheet moss rectangular tomato and grape baskets or oval mushroom baskets become dramatic and fanciful containers for food or plants, even without adding twig handles.

There are a variety of shrubby, pliable branches that make good handles. Old fashioned spirea or bridal wreath makes excellent handles. Low bush blueberry and black birch also work well. Always use *freshly cut, flexible branches that bend easily*. Dead wood will break, not bend.

You will need:

- green sheet moss to cover a shallow round 8 inch basket. About 24 inches square or several smaller pieces.

- 2 to 3 inch foam brush

- 1 pint white glue

- plastic container with lid to use as a glue pot

- five 12 inch lengths of light weights #24 or #28 florist wire

- two to four 15 to 20 inch twiggy stems with or without leaves

- florist shears or clippers

- inexpensive round basket 6 to 8 inches across

- raffia or ribbons for decorating

1. Cut two lengths of fresh heavily twigged branches. Remove any leaves you don't want.

2. Hold the basket in front of you. Look down into the center of it. Notice the skeleton or ribs that the basket is woven around. Choose a rib, it doesn't matter which one.

3. Lay the cut end of your branch inside the basket on top of your chosen rib. The bottom of the branch should be following the slight curve of the rib as it runs down the inside of the basket and flattens out to make the bottom of the basket.

4. Holding the bottom 2 or 3 inches of the branch firmly against the rib with one hand, take a l2 inch piece of florist wire and bend it into a

large U or hairpin shape.

5. Working from the inside of the basket near the bottom of the rib, place the ends of the wire on either side of the branch. Push the wire through the weave of the basket to the outside. Pull the wire tight around the base of the branch. Twist the wire sharply and tightly together just where it emerges from the basket. You should have two long ends of wire left.

6. Thread the two ends of wire back through the basket, one end emerging on either side of the branch. Twist them sharply and tightly together against the stem. Repeat the threading process, working the wire up the stem as you push and twist. You are literally tying or "shoe-lacing" your branch to the basket. Continue until you either run out of wire or run out of space.

7. If necessary, use a second piece of wire. Trim off any excess wire and tuck the sharp ends under the stem. Your handle should be tightly and firmly wired to the inside of the basket. No jiggling! Trace your rib to the opposite side of your basket. Wire a second shrubby branch firmly into place. *Following the rib ensures that your branches will be opposite each other.*

8. If you wish, add more bushiness to either side of the basket by wedging shorter pieces of twiggy branches into the wired stems. Add more wire if necessary. The handles should be firm and stable.

9. Complete your twiggy handle by pulling the tops of the branches together to form an arch. Gently weave as many twigs together as you can. Try to make the branches look as if they had grown into each other. Using short pieces of wire, gently wire your arch together in

one or two key places. Your handle can be as wild or tame as you like it.

10. Pour the glue into your glue pot and spread newspaper over your work surface. Gluing moss is messy business. Lay out the pieces of moss so you can see their size and shape. Shake the moss to remove excess dust and dirt. Pull off any thick pieces of bark or pebbles from the back of the moss. Arrange the placement of the moss in the basket so that the pieces always fold over the edge of the basket. *This is a key point. The edge of the basket will take the most wear and tear. To keep the moss from prematurely wearing away, never butt the pieces at the basket edge.*

11. Always begin gluing in the center of your basket. Use your largest and greenest pieces of moss there. Save smaller or browner pieces for the bottom of the basket. Moss glues very easily if you use enough glue. Lather the inside of your basket with glue. Take a piece of moss and press it firmly into place. Make a fist. Push firmly against the moss with the back of your fist. The moss must have full, strong contact with the glued basket in order to stick. If an edge or corner of the moss doesn't stick, lift up that section a little and lather in more glue. Moss acts as a sponge and absorbs a lot of glue.

12. Continue to lather sections of the basket with glue and press on moss. If a piece is too large for a space, tear it to fit. Don't cut moss. Cutting creates a straight edge that remains visible. By sliding the ragged edges of torn moss together, you can create the effect of one unbroken piece. Moss the bottom of the basket last.

Add raffia or ribbon bows, loops or streamers to the twig handle if you wish. You can also decorate the edges of the basket and part of the handle with dried flowers. Dip the stems or backs of the flowers into the glue and push into the moss.

If you are going to use your basket to hold a plant or flower arrangement, add a plastic container as a liner to keep the basket from getting wet.

Keep the basket out of direct sunlight to avoid fading—

Moss and Flower Baskets for the very Young

Little baskets covered with moss and glued-on flowers are a great spring project for young children and their parents. For the very youngest, parents need to help by attaching the twig handles. After that, the little ones can take over. They love lathering the glue onto the basket and then plopping on clumps of moss and gluing on flowers. The end result may not be beautiful to adult eyes but to the children they are just perfect!

CHAPTER FIFTEEN

Decorating Fairy Furniture

What could be more enchanting than a tiny armchair built of twigs, with a plumped cushion of soft green moss, feathery ferns growing up through the stretchers, and tiny pink roses twining through the back, with perhaps an acorn cup sitting on one arm? Wouldn't it make the perfect place for a garden fairy to spend a lazy summer afternoon sipping nectar and chatting with passing butterflies?

It's great fun to create such a fantasy. There are two ways to make fairy furniture. You can collect sturdy twigs, dried leaves, lichens and mushrooms and build your furniture from scratch, or you can purchase inexpensive twig furniture at one of the bargain-priced outlet stores and decorate it with mosses and dried flowers. I usually recommend beginning with the ready-made chairs and tables. Then, if you have become really intrigued, try to build your own.

First, find your furniture. There are twig tables, chairs, benches and loveseats widely available in craft shops, garden centers, and bargain chain stores. Most are between 4 and 8 inches high, perfect size for garden fairies to enjoy. the Once you have purchased your furniture, you will need:

- a small bag of green sheet moss.

- a small bag of Spanish moss.

- a selection of dried flowers ranging in size from tiny to l ½ inches across: roses, carnations, larkspur, ammobium, yarrows, pansies, delphinium, zinnias, lavender, blue salvia, xeranthium, straw flowers.

- a collection of natural materials from the woods or garden: dried leaves, seed cases and pods, pressed leaves and ferns, lichens, fungi, mushrooms, tiny pine cones, sparkling pebbles.

- white glue

- a shallow glue container

- 1 inch foam paintbrush

- newspaper

Directions

1. Spread your newspaper, then lay all your materials in groups around your piece of furniture. Pour your glue into the container.

2. Spend a minute or two just looking at your piece of furniture and all the materials you have collected for decorating. Try to imagine how you want your finished piece to look.

3. Begin decorating with the green sheet moss. Using the brush, thickly lather the glue on the areas of the furniture you want to upholster with moss. Press a piece of moss onto this thick layer of glue. Hold it firmly in place for a minute or two, then go on to your next piece of moss.

4. Once you feel you have enough sheet moss glued into place, begin adding leaves, lichen or other large, sturdy pieces. Lather glue on the back of each type of plant material and press firmly but gently into place. Allow some of the materials to overlap or even cover some of the moss.

5. Next attach the larger flowers. Working with one at a time, paint their backs with glue. Hold each one carefully but firmly onto the spot you want them to go for several seconds. When the first flower feels as if it is adhering, begin the second one.

6. The final step is to dip the stems or backs of the smaller flowers, one at a time, into the glue. Press each one gently into place.

Allow the decorated furniture to dry for 6 to 8 hours

Have fun!

RESOURCES

Books for Children and Their Adults to Enjoy

When you are deciding what books will work best in your family or classroom, remember to call you public library before you buy. The librarians will be happy to get you any book that interests you.

Fairies

Around the Year Elsa Beskow Floris

Children of the Forest Elsa Beskow Floris

Enchanted Gardens Katherine K. Schlosser Greensboro, North Carolina

Fairies and Chimneys Rose Flyeman Doubleday

Fairies and Friends Rose Flyeman Doubleday

Fairies and Magical Creatures Matthew Reinhart and Robert Sabuda Candlewick Press

Flower Fairy Series. Cicely Mary Barker Warne

Flowers' Festival Elsa Beskow Floris

Instructions Neil Gaiman Harper Collins

Peter in Blueberry Land Elsa Beskow Floris

Silver Pennies. Thompson, Blanche Jennings Macmillan

Tales from the Plant Kingdom Candace Miller Pourquoi Press

The Book of Fairy Poetry Michael Hague Harper Collins

The Story of the Rabbit Children Sibylle von Offers Floris

The Story of the Root Children Sibylle von Offers Floris

The Story of the Snow Children Sibylle von Offers Floris

The Story of the Wind Children Sibylle von Offers Floris

Woody, Hazel and Little Pip Elsa Beskow Floris

Gardening

A Blessing of Toads Sharon Lovejoy Hearst Books

Children and Gardens Gertrude Jekyll Antique Collectors Club

Garden Crafts for Kids Diane Rhoades Sterling/Lark Book

Gardening Is Easy Diana Simmons Arco Publishing

Gardening With Young Children Beatrys Lockie Hawthorne Press

Living Willow Sculpture John Warner Search Press

Muck and Magic Jo Readman Henry Doubleday Research Assoc.

Roots, Shoots, Buckets and Boots Sharon Lovejoy Hearst Books

Sunflower Houses Sharon Lovejoy
Interweave Press

Toad Cottages and Shooting Stars Sharon LovejoyWorkman

Fairy Festivals

Kids love parties and celebrations. These are all public events held by arboretums, botanic gardens herb shops and farms to celebrate plants, gardening and the natural world The dates given change each year, so be sure to check with any you might plan to attend for exact dates and schedule of events.

This list is by no means complete. Check in your local area for fairy and nature celebrations.

April

McKee Botanical Garden Vero beach, Florida

Spring Fairy Fest Tacoma, Washington

Village Herb Shop Chagrin Falls, Ohio

May

Blithewold Mansion, Gardens and Arboretum Bristol, Rhode Island

Spoutwood Farm May Fairie Fest Glen Rock, Pennsylvania

Maryland Faerie Fest Upper Marlbore, Mayrland

June

Summers Past Farm Fairy Festival Flinn Springs, California

Thistledown Greenhouse Faerie Festival Bonduel, Wisconsin

New York Fairy Festival Ouaguaga, New York

Enchanted Ground Fairy Festival Guelph, Ontario, Canada

San Diego Botanic Garden, Hamilton Children's Garden Fairy Day San Diego, California

Tizer Gardens Fairy and Wizard Festival Jefferson City, Montana

August

Fairy House Festival Coastal Maine Botanic Garden Boothbay, Maine

September

Rosemary House Fairy Festival Mechanicsburg, Pennsylvania

October

Fairy Fest Covington, Kentucky

Children's Gardens

Many public gardens, arboretums and botanic gardens have garden areas designed especially for children. Also libraries, some churches and many schools now have garden areas for children.

The following are a few well known gardens with especially wonderful gardens for children. Check in your area for others, then visit often. It's lots of fun for children and any adult lucky enough to go with them.

Coast of Maine Botanical garden Boothbay, Maine

Fernwood Botanic Garden and Nature Center Niles, Michigan

Ladew Topiary Gardens Monkdon, Maryland

Longwood Garden Kennet Square, Pennsylvania

Michigan 4-H Children's Garden East Lansing, Michigan

Hamilton Children's Garden, San Diego Botanic Garden San Diego, California

Winterthur Museum and Garden Winterthur, Delaware

Bibliography

Briggs, Katherine. *An Encyclopedia of Fairies.* New York: Pantheon, 1976.

The Fairies in Tradition and Literature. London:Routledge, 1967.

Hobberty Dick. London:Greenwillow, 1955.

The Personnel of Fairyland. London: Bentley, 1955.

The Vanishing People. New York: Pantheon, 1978.

Bunce, John T. *Fairytales, Their Origin and Meaning.* New York: Macmillan, 1878.

Clarkson, Rosetta. *Green Enchantment.* New York:Macmillan, 1940.

Dyer, T.F. Thiselton. *The Folklore of Plants.* New York: Appleton, 1889.

Ellacombe, Henry N. *Plantlore and Gardencraft of Shakespeare* London:W. Satchell, 1884

Friend, Hilderic. *Flower Lore.* Rockport, Mass.:Para Research, 1981. Reprint from *Flowers and Flower Lore,* 1884.

The Flowers and Their Story. London: Epworth.

Graves, Robert. *The White Goddess.* New York: Farrar, 1948, 1966.

Keightley, Thomas *Fairy Mythology, 2 vols*. London:Ainsworth, 1828.

The World Guide to Gnomes, Fairies, Elves and Other Little People. New York: Avenel, 1978.

Outhwaite, Ida Rentoul. *The Little World of Elves and Fairies*. Australia: Angus, 1985.

Quinn, Vernon. Leaves. *Their Place in Life and Legend*. London: Stokes, 1937.

Rohde, Eleanor Sinclair. *Shakespeare's Wild Flowers, Fairy Lore Gardens, Herbs, Gatherers of Simples and Bee Lore*. London: Medici, 1935.

Skinner, C.M. *Myths and Legends of Flowers*, Trees, *Fruits and Plants*. New York:Lippincott, 1925.

Spence, Lewis. *The Fairy Tradition in Britain*. London: Rider, 1948.

J.R.R Tolkien, *The Tolkien Reader*. New York: Ballentine Books, 1966

Wilde, Lady. *Irish Cures, Mystic charms and Superstition*. New York: Sterling , 1991

Betsy Williams has been growing, selling, decorating and teaching about living with herbs and flowers since 1972. Trained as a florist in Boston and England, she combines her floral and gardening skills with an extensive knowledge of history, plant lore and seasonal celebrations.

Her gardens, floral work and retail shop have been featured in many books, national magazines and newspapers.

Betsy created the first fairy festival at her retail shop in 1988, now replicated through out the world.

She is the author of several books on the uses and stories of herbs and flowers: *Potpourri and Fragrant Crafts* published by Readers Digest and *The Little Book Series,* a collection of books featuring ways to use herbs for their flavor, beauty and symbolism, published by The Proper Season Press.

She serves as Herb Chair for the Garden Club Federation of Massachusetts. Her column, *Living With Herbs* appears in their magazine, *Mayflower.*

She is a popular speaker at garden clubs, horticultural conferences, herb festivals and botanical gardens throughout the United States.

Other books from the
Proper Season Press

Mrs. Thrift Cooks
by Betsy Williams,
Illustrated by Ned Williams

Mrs. Thrift puts her herbal pantry to work. She shares her rules for food shopping and family cooking. Over 40 recipes using Mrs T's favorite condiments--herb mustard, herb vinegar, herb butter and rosemary walnuts--for fish, chicken, beef, lamb, pork, soups, vegetables and salads. $6.95

Mrs Thrift's Cupboard
by Betsy Williams,
Illustrated by Ned Williams

Betsy's fictional neighbor and good friend, Mrs. Thrift, helps herb and flower gardeners learn how to use their plants to enrich their daily lives. In this book, Mrs. Thrift shares her herbal tricks for recycling lovely leftovers from the refrigerator as well as her favorite recipes for herb flavored delights, such as Rosemary Walnuts and Garlic Wine, that can be given as gifts or used to enhance simple meals. Fun. Informative. Easy to use. $4.95